To my kids...each so precious to me

SIMON & SCHUSTER
First published in Great Britain in 2008 by Simon & Schuster UK Ltd
1ˢᵗ Floor, 222 Gray's Inn Road, London WC1X 8HB
A CBS Company

Originally published in 2008 by Simon & Schuster Books for Young Readers,
an imprint of Simon & Schuster Children's Publishing Division, New York

Book design by Alicia Mikles
The text for this book is set in Aunt Mildred
The illustrations for this book are rendered in pen and ink and watercolour

ISBN 978-1-84738-431-7

Printed in China 0119 APS

16 15 14 13 12

www.simonandschuster.co.uk

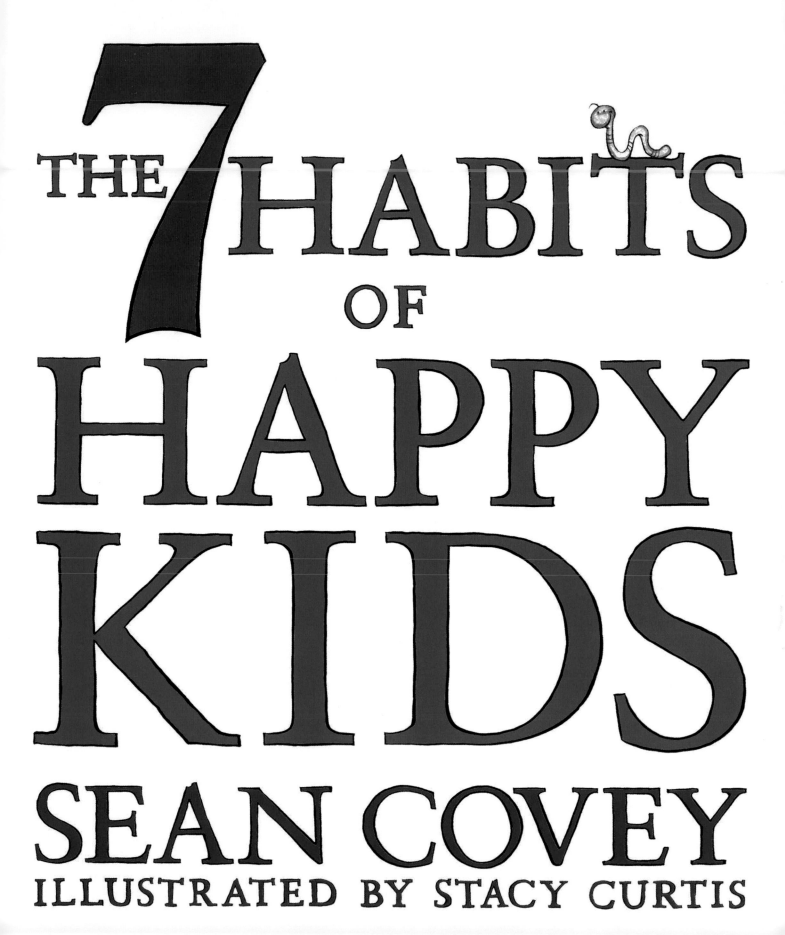

THE 7 HABITS OF HAPPY KIDS

SEAN COVEY
ILLUSTRATED BY STACY CURTIS

SIMON & SCHUSTER
LONDON • NEW YORK • SYDNEY • TORONTO

What's

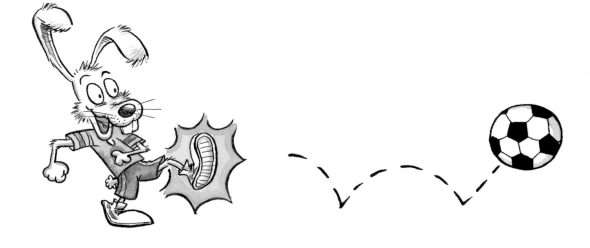

Inside

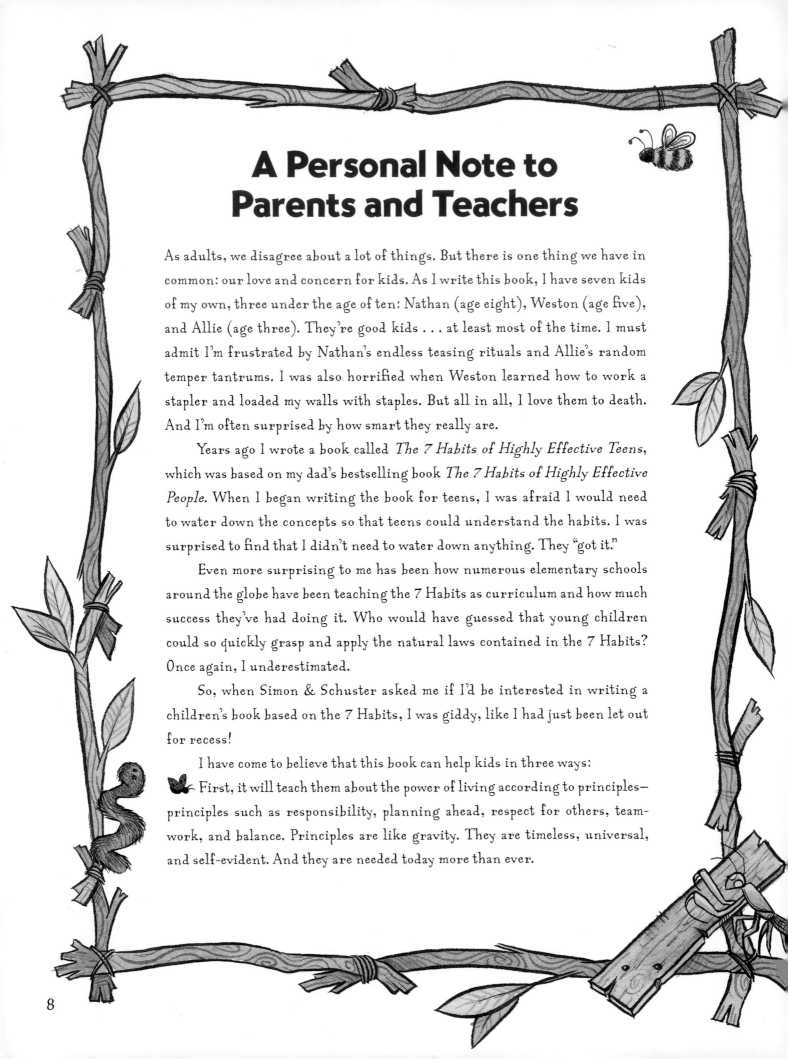

A Personal Note to Parents and Teachers

As adults, we disagree about a lot of things. But there is one thing we have in common: our love and concern for kids. As I write this book, I have seven kids of my own, three under the age of ten: Nathan (age eight), Weston (age five), and Allie (age three). They're good kids . . . at least most of the time. I must admit I'm frustrated by Nathan's endless teasing rituals and Allie's random temper tantrums. I was also horrified when Weston learned how to work a stapler and loaded my walls with staples. But all in all, I love them to death. And I'm often surprised by how smart they really are.

Years ago I wrote a book called *The 7 Habits of Highly Effective Teens,* which was based on my dad's bestselling book *The 7 Habits of Highly Effective People.* When I began writing the book for teens, I was afraid I would need to water down the concepts so that teens could understand the habits. I was surprised to find that I didn't need to water down anything. They "got it."

Even more surprising to me has been how numerous elementary schools around the globe have been teaching the 7 Habits as curriculum and how much success they've had doing it. Who would have guessed that young children could so quickly grasp and apply the natural laws contained in the 7 Habits? Once again, I underestimated.

So, when Simon & Schuster asked me if I'd be interested in writing a children's book based on the 7 Habits, I was giddy, like I had just been let out for recess!

I have come to believe that this book can help kids in three ways: First, it will teach them about the power of living according to principles—principles such as responsibility, planning ahead, respect for others, teamwork, and balance. Principles are like gravity. They are timeless, universal, and self-evident. And they are needed today more than ever.

Second, it will equip them with a common language they can use with parents and teachers. It can be so helpful to say, "I need to put first things first," or "Let's find a win-win for this situation," and for everyone to know exactly what is meant.

Third, whether they identify with Goob the Bear or Sophie Squirrel, kids will find part of themselves in one of these memorable characters. As a result, these stories will help kids apply the 7 Habits to their own lives.

As you page through this book, you'll notice that each story illustrates one habit. At the end of each story you'll find a note to parents and teachers (Parents' Corner), which has some suggestions on how to bring out the habit in that story. It also includes a list of questions to ask kids (Up for Discussion) and a list of small steps that kids may take (Baby Steps) to start practicing the habits. At the back of the book is a diagram of the 7 Habits that shows how they work together. And don't forget to visit the accompanying website at www.7HabitsKids.com. It has a lot of cool activities for kids, like quizzes, games, and printable character sketches that kids can color in themselves while they read the stories or are read to.

I join hands with you in our common and noble quest to help every kid be a happy kid!

All my best,
Sean Covey

Meet the Kids

Goob Bear

This is Goob the bear. He is the biggest kid in 7 Oaks—but he's also very friendly. He loves the outdoors and all kinds of bugs. Ants are his favorite bug.

Jumper Rabbit

Meet Jumper the rabbit. Jumper loves to play sports. He loves soccer, tennis, baseball, basketball, biking, swimming, and jumping—you name it. He also loves sneakers and owns all different kinds.

Lily Skunk

Lily is very crafty, especially for a skunk. She loves art. Lily spends most of her time drawing and painting and making all kinds of things. She also loves her little brother, Stink.

Sammy Squirrel

From the day Sammy was born, he has liked playing with gadgets and fixing things. You will never spot him without a tool or two. Sammy and his twin sister, Sophie, live in a tree house, as all squirrels do.

Sophie Squirrel

Sophie is Sammy's twin sister. Her very favorite thing to do in the world is read. She also loves math. Sometimes she uses really big words that she has to explain to all her friends.

Pokey Porcupine

Pokey has lots of pointy quills that show what kind of mood he is in. When Pokey is sad, the quills are droopy. When he is excited, they stand straight up. Pokey is really laid-back. He likes to lie around in his hammock all day and play his harmonica.

Tagalong Allie

And don't forget Tagalong Allie. She's a mouse. Allie likes to tag along with everyone in the gang, especially her best friend, Lily Skunk. Allie lives with her granny and loves to dress up in Granny's shoes and jewelry.

This is **Ernie the worm**. He is very shy, so you have to go looking for him. . . .

Bored! Bored! Bored!

Sammy Squirrel was bored, bored, BORED.

"Mom," he said, "I'm bored. There's nothing to do."

"How about all those gadgets you collect?" said Mom. "Broken toys, radios, cell phones. You love to tinker around with them."

"But I don't feel like it today," said Sammy. "Maybe Sophie can think up a fun thing for me to do."

Sammy knocked on Sophie's door. *Knock. Knock. Knock.* There was no answer.

"Sophie's gone to the library," said Mom. "She's
returning all those books she checked out last week.
And she'll probably bring a hundred more back to read."

"At least she's not bored," said Sammy.

"Well, you don't have to be bored either," said Mom.
"Why don't you see if Pokey can play?"

So off Sammy went to Pokey's house.

Pokey was lying in his hammock.

"Hiya, Pokey. Whatcha doin'?"

"What does it look like?" said Pokey. "I'm lying in my
hammock."

"I'm bored," said Sammy. "Can you think of something
fun for me to do?"

"Sure," said Pokey. "Try lying in my hammock."

"Ugh," said Sammy. "That sounds even more boring."

"I don't think it is," said Pokey. "But if you do, why don't you see what Lily's doing?"

So off Sammy went to Lily's house.

Lily was in her playroom, painting a picture.

"Hi, Lily," said Sammy. "I'm bored. Can you think of something fun for me to do?"

"You bet!" said Lily. "You can help me paint Dottie Doll, and then we can make frames out of red paper or maybe you could paint my tail."

"Ugh," said Sammy. "I don't feel like painting. Can't you think of something else that's fun to do?"

"Nope," said Lily. "I like painting. Why don't you see what Goob's up to?"

So off Sammy went to Goob's house.

Goob had his magnifying glass out and was looking at something in the grass.

"Hey, Goob," said Sammy. "Whatcha doin'?"

"Ants!" said Goob. "I'm looking at ants!"

Goob pulled Sammy down next to him. He shoved the magnifying glass into his paws. "Lean down and you'll see hundreds of them. They're so cool!"

Sammy looked through the glass. "Yikes!" he said. "I don't want to look at ants. They're creepy. Can't you think of something else that's fun for me to do?"

"Can't," said Goob. "I'm into ants right now. Why don't you see what Jumper's up to?"

So off Sammy went to Jumper's house.

Jumper was shooting baskets in the driveway.

He dribbled the ball over to Sammy. "Want to get in the game?" he asked.

"No," said Sammy. "I don't feel like playing basketball. Can't you think of something fun for me to do?"

"Watch this," said Jumper. "I'm the rabbit!" He jumped up and stuffed the ball into the basket. "A slam dunk!"

Sammy sighed. Nobody seemed to have any fun ideas. Maybe he could play with Tagalong Allie. So off he went to her house.

Allie's Granny was painting the front porch.

"Hi, Granny," said Sammy. "Where's Tagalong Allie?"

"She's in bed with a sore throat," said Granny.

"Bummer," said Sammy. He paused. "I'm bored. Do you want to play?"

Allie's Granny laughed. "Can't, Sammy Squirrel. I'm busy."

"No one will help me have fun," complained Sammy. "I'm *so* bored."

"Well, isn't that *your* fault?" asked Allie's Granny. "You're in charge of having fun, not somebody else."

"What do you mean?" asked Sammy.

"I mean, you can make your own fun. You don't need others to make it happen. Just look around and think about it. You'll find something fun to do."

Sammy looked around. He saw clouds. He saw trees. He saw three garbage cans lined up against the house. One had an old radio on top, with wires sticking out in all directions.

Suddenly Sammy's brain lit up like a flashlight.

"Do you want that old radio anymore?" he asked Allie's
Granny.

"No," she said. "It's broken. That's why I threw it away."

"Can I have it?" asked Sammy. "I love radios!"

"Why, sure," said Allie's Granny.

Sammy picked up the radio, carried it home, and set
it down on the floor of his room. Then he got started. It
took him a few hours to get the radio to work again, but
by lunchtime it was fixed. He tied some ribbons around it
and pasted stars all over. Then he carried the radio back to
Tagalong Allie's house.

"What do we have here?" asked Allie's Granny.

"A get-well present for Allie!" said Sammy. "I fixed it so she can listen to the radio while she's getting over her sore throat. I'm not bored anymore. I finally figured out how to make my own fun."

"Great!" said Allie's Granny. "Let's go inside and show Allie."

When Allie saw the radio, she broke into a smile as wide as a slice of cantaloupe.

"I wuv da wibbons!" she said.

PARENTS' CORNER
Habit 1—Be Proactive • *You're in Charge*

I can't count how many times my kids have whined, "Dad, we're so bored. There's nothing to do," as if their boredom were somehow my fault. I'll respond with something like, "So what are you going to do about it?" This usually keeps them out of my hair—at least for a little while. My point is: It's vital to teach kids to take responsibility for their own lives, for their own fun or boredom, for their own happiness or unhappiness. This is Habit 1—Be Proactive. In other words, take charge of your own life and stop playing the victim.

In this story, you may want to point out to the kids how Sammy tries to blame everyone else—his mom, his friends, life in general—for his boredom. He wants someone to fix his problem and to help him have fun. After talking with Allie's Granny, he finally figures out that he's in charge of making his own fun, and he makes it happen.

Up for Discussion

1. Why was Sammy bored?
2. Whose fault was it that Sammy was bored? Was it Sophie's fault? Pokey's? Lily's? Goob's? Jumper's? Granny's? Or somebody else's?
3. What did Allie's Granny teach Sammy about having fun?
4. Do you ever feel bored? If so, what can you do about it?
5. Who is in charge of the choices you make: you or somebody else?

Baby Steps

1. The next time you feel bored, do something nice for someone else, like Sammy did for Allie.
2. Try doing something today that you've always been scared to do. Make a new friend, raise your hand in class, or clean the toilet.
3. The next time you get mad and want to say something mean or rude, bite your tongue instead and don't say it.
4. If you do something wrong, say you're sorry before someone asks you to apologize.

Goob and the Bug-Collecting Kit

Goob was walking by Tootle's Toy Store when he saw a bug-collecting kit in the window. It was on sale for four dollars.

"Wow!" said Goob. "I've wanted a kit like that for a loooong time. But I don't have four dollars. I need to earn it. I need to come up with a plan."

Goob went home and wrote out a list.

GooB'2 GoALS
1. SAVE SoME $.
2. Buy Bug-Collecting Kit.
3. Buy preSENt for ALLie's BirtHday.
4. Buy Pizza witH HoNey on top.
5. Go to MoviE.

Just then, Jumper stopped by.

"What's that, Goob?"

"I'm making a list of things I want to do," said Goob.

"Wow! Can I be part of your game plan?" asked Jumper.

"Sure," said Goob. "I have a great idea—let's sell lemonade. It's really hot out and folks will want a cold drink."

That afternoon, Goob and Jumper set up their lemonade stand.

Sammy and Sophie were the first to stop by.

"Lemonade!" said Sammy. "I'll buy a cup."

"Me too," said Sophie. "This heat is oppressive."

Goob and Jumper looked at each other.

"I have no idea what you just said," said Jumper.

"Hot," said Sophie. "It's really hot!"

Next, Lily Skunk and Tagalong Allie stopped by.

"I'll buy a cup for Tagalong Allie and two cups for me," said Lily. "And then Allie and I are going to my house to color—isn't that right, Allie?"

"Wite," said Allie.

After a few hours, Goob and Jumper had sold all their lemonade. They had made twenty dollars.

"Wow, we're rich!" said Goob. "Let's divide it up. Here's ten dollars for you and ten dollars for me."

"Home run!" said Jumper. "I know just what I'm going to spend my money on." And off he ran to Tootle's Toy Store.

Jumper bought two candy bars, some bubble gum, and a bag of popcorn, which he ate right away.

He then got himself a cheap yo-yo, which broke after three tries,

and a small squirt gun, which he lost on his way home.

Meanwhile, Goob went home and read over his list. He put one dollar in a jar for savings.

Next, he went to
Tootle's and bought
the bug-collecting
kit for four dollars.

He spent two dollars on a little mirror
for Tagalong Allie's birthday present.

On his way home, he stopped at
Penny's Place and bought himself
a slice of honey pizza for one dollar.

He still had two dollars left to go to a movie.
As Goob was walking along, Jumper caught up to him.

"Where ya headed, Goob?" he asked.

"To the movies," said Goob.

"I wish I could go," said Jumper with a sigh. "But I've spent all my money."

"On what?" asked Goob.

"Lots of stuff," said Jumper. "My money just kind of disappeared."

"You should have planned ahead," said Goob. "I was able to get everything on my list."

Jumper's ears and whiskers drooped. "I guess I dropped the ball," he said.

"Don't let it bug you," said Goob. "Now you know what to do next time."

"Aww, you're smart," said Jumper. "Have fun at the movie."

"You can have fun too," said Goob. "I have two dollars left—enough for both of us to go to the dollar movie. *The Giant Spider Eats the Blob* is showing. Come on, let's go!"

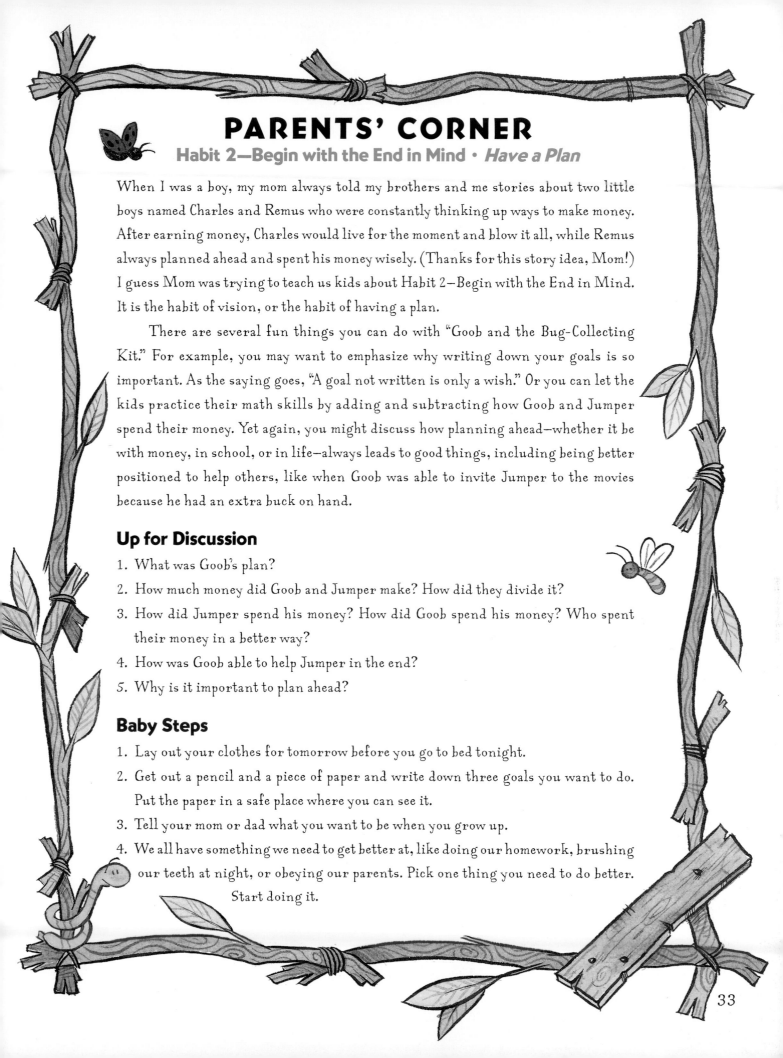

PARENTS' CORNER
Habit 2—Begin with the End in Mind · *Have a Plan*

When I was a boy, my mom always told my brothers and me stories about two little boys named Charles and Remus who were constantly thinking up ways to make money. After earning money, Charles would live for the moment and blow it all, while Remus always planned ahead and spent his money wisely. (Thanks for this story idea, Mom!) I guess Mom was trying to teach us kids about Habit 2—Begin with the End in Mind. It is the habit of vision, or the habit of having a plan.

There are several fun things you can do with "Goob and the Bug-Collecting Kit." For example, you may want to emphasize why writing down your goals is so important. As the saying goes, "A goal not written is only a wish." Or you can let the kids practice their math skills by adding and subtracting how Goob and Jumper spend their money. Yet again, you might discuss how planning ahead—whether it be with money, in school, or in life—always leads to good things, including being better positioned to help others, like when Goob was able to invite Jumper to the movies because he had an extra buck on hand.

Up for Discussion

1. What was Goob's plan?
2. How much money did Goob and Jumper make? How did they divide it?
3. How did Jumper spend his money? How did Goob spend his money? Who spent their money in a better way?
4. How was Goob able to help Jumper in the end?
5. Why is it important to plan ahead?

Baby Steps

1. Lay out your clothes for tomorrow before you go to bed tonight.
2. Get out a pencil and a piece of paper and write down three goals you want to do. Put the paper in a safe place where you can see it.
3. Tell your mom or dad what you want to be when you grow up.
4. We all have something we need to get better at, like doing our homework, brushing our teeth at night, or obeying our parents. Pick one thing you need to do better. Start doing it.

Pokey and the Spelling Test

One Monday, Pokey sat in class watching Ms. Hoot write six words on the blackboard:

    play   fun   have   for   you   drum

"These words will be on Friday's spelling test," said Ms. Hoot. "Be sure you study every night, and then you'll spell these words just right!"

After school, Pokey went home and took a nap.

Ding-dong! Someone was at the door. It was Sammy.

"Hiya, Pokey," said Sammy. "Do you want to go to the dump and look for some gadgets?"

Pokey knew he should study, but going to the dump
sounded like more fun.

"Sure," said Pokey.

When they got there, Pokey saw an old drum. He
thumped it lightly.

Dum-dum-duuuuuum-dum.

"Awesome!" said Pokey. He carried the drum home. He
played it for the rest of the afternoon.

On Tuesday, Lily Skunk and Tagalong Allie stopped by Pokey's house.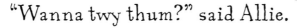

"Allie and I just made some chocolate-chip cookies. They're *sooooo* yummy," said Lily.

"Wanna twy thum?" said Allie.

"What?" said Pokey.

"Do you wanna try some?" said Lily.

"I have to study for my spelling test," said Pokey. "But . . . I guess I can do that later." So off he went to Lily's house.

When Pokey got back, he played his drum. Then he played his harmonica. Then he fell asleep.

On Wednesday afternoon, Pokey went on a butterfly hunt with Goob.

And on Thursday afternoon, he took a bicycle ride with Jumper. When he got home, he remembered that the spelling test was the next day and he hadn't studied even one word. He took out his spelling cards. He taped them to the wall.

play   fun   have   for   you   drum

Pokey tried to write them down, but the letters swam in front of him like fish.

There were too many words to learn in just one night. The more Pokey tried to memorize them, the more confused he got. He finally gave up and went to sleep.

The next day, Pokey failed the test. He spelled every word wrong except for *drum*.

"What happened?" asked Ms. Hoot. "Didn't you study? I know you could have done better."

"I kept finding other things to do," said Pokey.

Sophie was standing nearby. "You shouldn't procrastinate," she said.

"Huh?" said Pokey.

"I mean, you should have put first things first," said Sophie. "Done your homework first, then had fun later."

Ms. Hoot agreed. She told Pokey he could take the test again next Friday.

"And this time, don't wing it!" she said.

Pokey went home.
He looked at his new drum.
Dum-dum-duuuuuuum-dum
he heard in his head.

He looked at his spelling words.

Ding-dong. Someone was at the door. It was Sophie.

"I came to help you study," she said.

They worked for a whole hour without stopping once.

Ding-dong. Someone else was at the door. It was Jumper.

"Wanna play baseball?" he said.

"Can't, Jumper," said Pokey. "I'm studying."

"You're *what*?"

"Studying," said Pokey.

"That's cool," said Jumper.

"Catch you another time."

And off he ran.

Pokey studied a little bit each day. On Friday, he took the test again. "Fur and feathers!" said Ms. Hoot. "You got a perfect score!"

Pokey's quills poked out all over! He wanted to thank Sophie. He went home and got his drum. He took it to her house and left it with a note.

PARENTS' CORNER
Habit 3—Put First Things First • *Work First, Then Play*

It's funny how kids will spend thirty minutes complaining about their chores, not realizing they could have completed them in the same amount of time they spent complaining. Go figure. Indeed, putting first things first is hard. In fact, of all the habits, it's the hardest one to keep. Why? Because we're all somewhat addicted to doing the urgent thing or the easier thing first. Yet if we don't teach our kids to delay gratification and do the hard thing (or first thing) first while they are young, they may learn too late or not at all. In this story, be sure to point out how awful it can feel when you procrastinate and put things off, like when Pokey crammed the night before the test. Contrast that with how good it feels when you are prepared. As a wise person once put it, "Do what you have to do so you can do what you want to do."

Up for Discussion

1. Why did Pokey put off studying for his spelling test? What did he do instead?
2. How did Pokey feel the night before the first test?
3. What does *procrastinate* mean? What did Sophie teach Pokey about procrastination?
4. How did Pokey feel after he studied all week and aced his spelling test?
5. Why is it so important to put first things first?

Baby Steps

1. What are some of your most important jobs or responsibilities? Practicing the piano? Making your bed? Doing your homework? Taking out the garbage? Talk about them with your mom or dad.
2. Tomorrow surprise your parents and do your chores before they even ask.
3. The next time you have a lot of homework to do, do the hardest part first.
4. Think of something you've been putting off for a long time, like cleaning up your room, pumping up that tire on your bike, or fixing that broken dresser drawer. Go do it right now!

Lily Plants
a Garden

When Lily Skunk was just a little skunk, she loved to visit Ms. Hoot's garden. There were so many amazing vegetables to look at—cucumbers, radishes, carrots, peppers, beans, and lettuce.

One afternoon, Lily said to her mom, "I wish we had a vegetable garden like Ms. Hoot's."

"Me too," said Mom, "but planting a garden takes a lot of time and effort."

"I know, but I'll do all the work," said Lily. "I promise."

"I'm sorry," said Mom. "I just don't think you realize how much work it takes. You have to fix the dirt, then plant the seeds, then weed and water almost every day. I bet I'd end up doing most of it, and I'm just too busy right now."

"But I really, really, really want a garden," said Lily.

Lily looked as if she might burst into tears.

"Well," said Mom, looking at Lily's face, "maybe someday we could look into planting something easier . . . something

like . . . a strawberry patch. A strawberry patch wouldn't take as much work as a vegetable garden . . . and strawberries are so delicious!"

But Lily didn't want to wait 'til some day. She wanted a vegetable garden right now.

In the middle of the night, Lily woke up with a great idea. She ran over to her desk and pulled out a sheet of paper. She got her favorite pen and wrote a note to her mom:

Dear Mom,
If you will let me have a garden,
here's what I'll do:
☆ Grow vegetables AND strawberries
☆ Water and weed
☆ Get Stink to help
Here's what you'll get:
☆ Not much work for you
☆ Yummy vegetables and tasty
strawberries.
Love,
♡ Lily ♡

47

The next morning, Lily ran downstairs and handed her note to Mom.

"Oh, Lily," Mom said as she read it. "I can see that you want this garden *very* badly." She paused. Then she said, "Well, if you promise to do most of the work and I get to eat strawberries, I'd say your plan is a win-win. When do you want to get started?"

"Right now!" said Lily.

That afternoon, Mom and Lily raked the dirt and planted the seeds. Dad put up a scarecrow. After that, Mom and Dad got busy with other things, and Lily kept working in the garden.

All summer long, Lily watered and weeded, weeded and watered, just like she promised. It was hard work. Stink helped too—at least he tried, but usually he only got in the way. He kept watering himself instead of watering the vegetables.

And Lily had to remind him not to pull up the carrots to see how they were doing.

Soon tiny plants poked up from the dirt.

After several more weeks, Lily started to see some vegetables—and strawberries, too.

When everything was ready to harvest, Lily and Stink
picked a whole bunch of vegetables and strawberries and
brought them into the house.

"Wow!" said Mom. "Fresh vegetables and strawberries!
That's great! Now I won't have to buy veggies and
strawberries at the store anymore. And it's so healthy to eat
out of our own garden! What a treat!"

That night for dinner, Lily, Stink, Mom, and Dad had vegetable soup and strawberry shortcake.

"These strawberries are sooooo juicy," said Mom. "They are delicious *and* nutritious. I'm sure proud of you, Lily! You worked really hard all summer long, and I hardly did a thing, just like you said. And thank you, too, Stink!"

"I'm glad you're happy," said Lily.

"Hey, maybe I should plant a flower garden," said Mom.

"Are you sure you want to do that, Mom?" asked Lily. "Planting a garden takes a lot of time and effort. You just don't realize how much work it takes!"

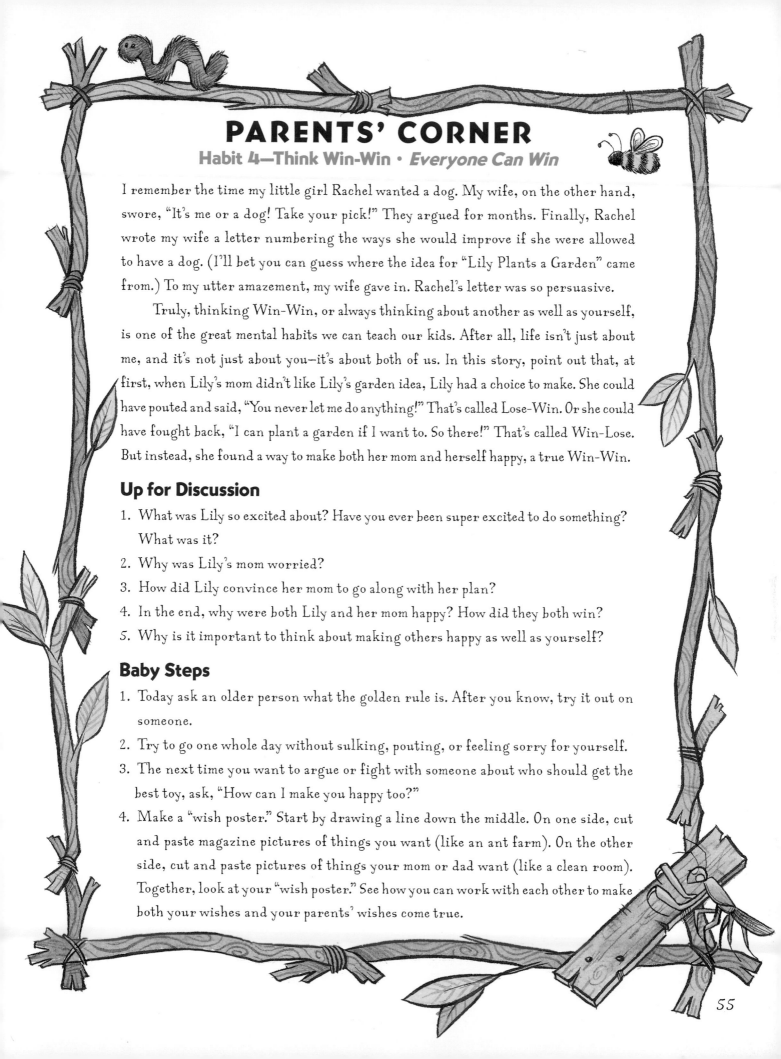

PARENTS' CORNER
Habit 4—Think Win-Win • *Everyone Can Win*

I remember the time my little girl Rachel wanted a dog. My wife, on the other hand, swore, "It's me or a dog! Take your pick!" They argued for months. Finally, Rachel wrote my wife a letter numbering the ways she would improve if she were allowed to have a dog. (I'll bet you can guess where the idea for "Lily Plants a Garden" came from.) To my utter amazement, my wife gave in. Rachel's letter was so persuasive.

Truly, thinking Win-Win, or always thinking about another as well as yourself, is one of the great mental habits we can teach our kids. After all, life isn't just about me, and it's not just about you—it's about both of us. In this story, point out that, at first, when Lily's mom didn't like Lily's garden idea, Lily had a choice to make. She could have pouted and said, "You never let me do anything!" That's called Lose-Win. Or she could have fought back, "I can plant a garden if I want to. So there!" That's called Win-Lose. But instead, she found a way to make both her mom and herself happy, a true Win-Win.

Up for Discussion

1. What was Lily so excited about? Have you ever been super excited to do something? What was it?

2. Why was Lily's mom worried?

3. How did Lily convince her mom to go along with her plan?

4. In the end, why were both Lily and her mom happy? How did they both win?

5. Why is it important to think about making others happy as well as yourself?

Baby Steps

1. Today ask an older person what the golden rule is. After you know, try it out on someone.

2. Try to go one whole day without sulking, pouting, or feeling sorry for yourself.

3. The next time you want to argue or fight with someone about who should get the best toy, ask, "How can I make you happy too?"

4. Make a "wish poster." Start by drawing a line down the middle. On one side, cut and paste magazine pictures of things you want (like an ant farm). On the other side, cut and paste pictures of things your mom or dad want (like a clean room). Together, look at your "wish poster." See how you can work with each other to make both your wishes and your parents' wishes come true.

Jumper and the Lost Butterfly Net

One day Jumper stopped by Goob's.

"Wanna play Frisbee?" he asked.

"No, thanks," said Goob. "I'm too sad, because I lost my butterfly net."

"But it's a sunny day," said Jumper. "We could go play at Fish-Eye Lake."

"I don't feel like it," said Goob.

"Please?" said Jumper. "It would be so much fun. Come on, let's go." He started bouncing in circles around Goob.

"No!" said Goob. "You're talking too much and you're moving too much and you never listen! You go ahead and have fun without me."

"Okay," said Jumper. "Catch you later."

Jumper ran off. He jogged by Tagalong Allie's house. She was sitting in her sandbox.

"Wah! Wah!" cried Allie.

"What's wrong?" called Jumper.

"Me thweter back woods."

"Huh?" said Jumper. "You want to get wet? Okay, let's go swimming."

Allie shook her head. "Wah! Wah!" she cried. "ME THWETER BACK WOODS!"

"Oh, I get it," said Jumper. "Woods. You want to go play in the woods."

Allie kicked her legs against the sand. "WAHHHHHH! WAHHHHHH! ME THWETER BACKWOODS!"

"I give up," said Jumper. "Let's see if Lily Skunk can figure out what's wrong."

Jumper picked up Allie and carried her to Lily's house.

He rang the doorbell.

Lily came to the door. "Hi, Jumper. Hi, Allie. What's up?"

"WAH! WAH!" cried Allie.

Lily looked at her. "What's the matter?" she asked.

"ME THWETER BACK WOODS!"

"Oh, dear," said Lily. "Your sweater's on backwards! You poor thing!"

Lily pulled off Allie's sweater, turned it around, and put it back on her.

"How'd you figure that out?" said Jumper.

"You have to listen with your heart and your eyes, not just your ears," said Lily. "Didn't you see that her sweater was on backwards?"

"No," said Jumper. "That passed right by me."

He was quiet for a moment. "I gotta go see Goob."

Jumper ran off.

"Wait fur meee!" yelled Allie.

They found Goob hunched over on a log in front of his house.

"I can now see you're really sad," said Jumper. "What's wrong?"

"I already told you," said Goob. "I lost my butterfly net. It's only my favorite thing in the whole wide world."

"Well, come on. Let's look for it!" said Jumper.

"I've *been* looking for it," said Goob. "It's gone. Lost. Forever."

Allie tugged at Jumper's shorts.

"Wiwee's twee," she said.

"Huh?" said Jumper. "Come again?"

He leaned over and looked Allie right in the eyes.

"Butterfwy net by Wiwee's twee," Allie repeated.

"Wiwee's twee?" said Jumper. "Oh, I get it. Lily's tree! Goob's butterfly net is at the Great Oak Tree by Lily's house! Is that it?"

"Yeth!" said Allie.

"Good girl!" said Jumper. "Let's go find it!"

They all ran back to Lily's house. The butterfly net was leaning against the Great Oak Tree in front of her house.

"My butterfly net!" yelled Goob.

He ran over and grabbed it. "Now I remember. I was chasing butterflies here yesterday. How'd you figure out what Allie was saying, Jumper?"

"You have to listen with your eyes and heart, not just your ears," said Jumper.

"Hmmm," said Goob.

"Wanna pway in my than boxth?" asked Allie.

Goob leaned over and looked at Allie.

"Say what?" asked Goob.

"Wanna pway in my than boxth?" said Allie.

"I think I get what you're saying now," said Goob. "You want us to play in your sandbox. Is that right?"

Allie gave a big, wide smile.

"Come on, Jumper," said Goob. "Let's all go!"

PARENTS' CORNER
Habit 5—Seek First to Understand, Then to Be Understood
• Listen Before You Talk

My wife and I have nicknames for our kids. We named Allie, age three, "Scream" because that's what she does. When she doesn't get her way or feel heard, she screams. Loud! It is her way of getting attention. As adults, we may not scream, but we act out in other ways when we don't feel that anyone is listening. For sure, the deepest need of the human heart is to be understood.

In school we're taught how to read, write, and speak. But we're not taught how to listen, which is the most important communication skill of all. Listening with our ears isn't good enough, because less than 10 percent of communication is contained in the words we use. The rest comes from body language and the tone and feeling reflected in our voice. What a great blessing it would be if we could teach our kids how to listen while they're young! Use this story to point out how Jumper learned to listen, not only with his ears but also with his eyes and his heart—and as a result, everyone was happier.

Up for Discussion

1. What did Jumper do when Goob told him he was sad and didn't want to play?
2. How did Allie feel when Jumper couldn't understand her? How do you feel when no one understands you?
3. Who helped Allie solve her problem? What did Lily Skunk say to Jumper about listening?
4. Who was happy at the end of the story? Why is listening so important?

Baby Steps

1. Try to go one whole hour without talking even once. Instead, just watch the people around you and listen to what they are saying. Good luck!
2. Think of someone in your life who you think is a good listener. Your grandma? Your dad? Your best friend? What do they do that makes them a good listener?
3. The next time one of your friends is sad, notice her eyes or the way he holds his body. Tell them you know they are sad and you want to help.

The Big Bad Badgers

On Saturdays, the friends often got together to play soccer at Uncle Bud's Park. Sometimes they would have pickup games with whoever else showed up.

One day the Big Bad Badgers came to the park.

"Wanna play soccer?" the biggest Badger asked. "We'll beat you, but we'll play you 'cause there's no one else around."

The friends huddled together.

"They'll squash us like bugs," said Goob.

"Yeah, I'm outta here," said Pokey.

"I'm going home to paint," said Lily.

"Wait," said Sophie. "They may look big and scary, but we're experienced. We can beat them. And Jumper will score lots of goals."

"We'll show them who's boss," said Jumper.

It took some work, but Sophie and Jumper finally convinced the others to play.

But before the team even knew what had happened, the Badgers had scored three points.

TOGETHER
EVERYONE
ACHIEVES
MORE!

Jumper tried hard to shoot, but none of the gang would pass the ball to him.

Sophie and Sammy kept tripping over their tails.

Lily stopped to pick flowers.

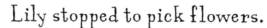

Pokey lay down and took a nap.

Goob took out his magnifying glass to look for ants.

Allie finally scored a goal, but it was for the other team.

The Badgers now had four points!

"This is a waste of time," said one of the Badgers. "We're going home."

"Wait a minute," said Jumper. "I need to talk to my team."

He called his team to the sidelines.

"We can still win this game," he said.

"Forget it," said Pokey. "They'll turn us into mashed potatoes."

"No!" said Sophie. "They may be bigger and stronger than us, but we can beat them if we play as a team. Let's use our assets."

"Our what?" asked Lily.

"Our strengths," said Sophie. "Pokey, you play goalie and stick out your quills to scare those nasty Badgers. Jumper, just keep shooting, since that's what you're good at. Sammy, use your big bushy tail to pass the ball. Lily, when you're not picking flowers, you're great at headers, you know. Goob, you're huge, so just get in their way. Allie, you did a good job—now just head for the right goal this time. Come on, guys. Let's be a team!"

Everyone agreed to try Sophie's idea.

"Stick around," said Jumper to the Badgers. "We're back in the game."

"Nothing's gonna change," said the meanest Badger. "You'll see."

The two teams faced off.
Jumper passed the ball to Sophie.

Sophie passed it to Lily.

Lily headed it to Sammy.

Sammy used his tail
to push it to Jumper.

Jumper kicked
the ball into the goal.

"Goal!" yelled Goob.

Now the team was really excited. Lily headed the ball to Sammy, who scored another point. Pokey stuck out his quills whenever the Badgers came close. Goob used his big body to get in  the way of the forwards. Jumper and Sophie scored two more points. The game was tied, 4-4, and both teams were getting tired.

"Let's keep going 'til someone scores the winning point!" yelled Jumper.

"I just thought of a really original play," said Sophie.

"Come again?" said Goob.

"A play that's never been tried before," said Sophie. She huddled with the team and explained her idea.

"Let's go for it!" said Jumper.

The next time they had the ball, they tried out Sophie's idea. Goob passed the ball to Lily. Lily headed it to Sammy. Sammy looked for Jumper, but Jumper was guarded by several Badgers.

From the corner of his eye, Sammy saw that Allie was free.

"Me, me, meeeee!" shouted Allie.

Sammy kicked the ball to her. Just as a Badger charged Allie, she dove through his legs and got the ball.

But as she ran for the goal, she tripped.

"Oops," said Allie as she fell flat on her face. Yet somehow the ball caught the side of her head. *BOINK!* The ball sailed into the goal for the winning point.

"We won!" screamed the gang. "Hooray for Allie!"

Goob lifted Allie up onto his shoulders.

"Good game," said the Badgers' captain. "You guys were better than I thought!"

"Thanks!" said Jumper. "Let's play again sometime."

"Sure," said the captain, "as long as Allie plays on our team!"

PARENTS' CORNER
Habit 6—Synergize · *Together Is Better*

Often in my home after a family meal, we have what we call a "fifteen-minute program." For fifteen minutes everyone drops what they're doing and we do the dishes together. I'm always amazed at how quickly we can do all the dishes and put everything away when we work as a team. That's what synergy is: valuing differences and then working together to create a better solution than what anyone could do alone. It's when 1 + 1 = 3 or more.

As you read this story with your kids, be sure to highlight how the 7 Oaks gang used synergy to win the game. Working alone, they couldn't score even one goal against the Badgers. But once they started focusing on each kid's unique strengths and began playing as a team, they were unstoppable. It's just as Helen Keller once said: "Alone we can do so little; together we can do so much."

Up for Discussion

1. Why didn't the 7 Oaks gang want to play the Badgers in a soccer game at first?
2. Why did the gang get so far behind by halftime? And why did they want to quit?
3. What strengths did Sophie tell Allie, Goob, Jumper, Sammy, Lily, and Pokey that each of them had? What are you good at?
4. How did the gang win the game? What made the difference? Who scored the winning goal?
5. How does it feel when you win as a team?

Baby Steps

1. Write down three things that you're really good at. Then write down three things that someone else you know is good at, like your brother or sister or a friend.
2. Watch your favorite sports team play a game. Pay extra attention to how all the players work together as a team.
3. Talk about what makes a bad team member and what makes a good team member.
4. This summer, call two friends and put up a lemonade stand, just like Goob and Jumper did in the story "Goob and the Bug-Collecting Kit." One person can create the poster, one can make the lemonade, and one can set up the table and bring the cups and ice. Have fun!

Sleepy Sophie

One sunny day at Mountainville Elementary, while Ms. Hoot was teaching about the letter Z, Sophie fell fast asleep.

Ms. Hoot walked over and gently tickled her with a feather. "Wake up, Sophie," she said.

Sophie opened her eyes. She blinked, trying to remember where she was.

"Didn't you get enough sleep last night?" asked Ms. Hoot.

"I guess not," said Sophie. She yawned. "I'll go to bed early tonight."

On the way home from school, Sammy said, "Wow, sis, I can't believe you fell asleep in class today. That was *sooooo* embarrassing."

"I know," said Sophie. "But I'm feeling so fatigued."

"Fatigued?" asked Sammy.

"Tired," said Sophie. "I've been feeling very tired lately."

"Duh! That's 'cause you stay up all night reading under the covers. Mom should take your flashlight away."

"But reading is the spice of life," said Sophie.

"I didn't know books were spicy," said Sammy. "I just thought Mexican food was."

"Never mind," said Sophie, rolling her eyes. "Let's just hurry home so I can take a nap."

When they got to their tree, Sophie lay down on the couch. Then she saw a book. She just *had* to pick it up.

Knock. Knock.

Lily was at the door. "Want to color?" she asked. "I have some new coloring books."

"No, thanks," said Sophie. "I'm exhausted. Maybe tomorrow we could color."

"Okay," said Lily. "I'm off to Allie's."

After Lily left, Sophie picked up her book again.

Knock. Knock.

Sophie sighed. Jumper was at the door.

"Wanna ride bikes?" he asked.

"No, thanks," said Sophie. "I don't have any energy."

"That's terrible," said Jumper. "You need vitamins."

"I need a nap," said Sophie.

"Gotcha," said Jumper. "I'll come by tomorrow and see if you've bounced back."

Jumper dashed off and Sophie picked up her book AGAIN.

Knock. Knock.

Pokey was at the door.

"I've learned to play a new tune," he said. "Let's walk to Fish-Eye Lake and you can lie down and look at the sky while I play it for you."

"I don't have time for that," said Sophie. "I'm busy reading."

"You can't read ALL the time," said Pokey. "Sometimes you just gotta listen to music and look at the clouds."

"Maybe another time," said Sophie.

"Okay," said Pokey. "See ya around."

Pokey left and Sophie picked up her book again. But before she knew it, she was fast asleep.

When it was time for
dinner, Sophie's mother
shook her awake.

"You've been asleep a
long time," said Mom. She
touched Sophie's forehead.
"Do you feel okay?"

"I'm just kind of worn-out," said Sophie.

"Hmmm," said Mom. "I think you're spending too much
time reading. Reading is a great thing, but you need balance
in your life. You need to find things that don't just have to do
with your mind."

"What else is there?" asked Sophie.

"There's your heart, your body, and your soul," said Mom.

"Tell me more," said Sophie.

"Well, you use your heart when you play with your friends," said Mom.

"And my body?" asked Sophie.

"You use your body when you exercise."

"And my soul?" asked Sophie.

"You use your soul when you find something quiet to do that makes you feel fresh inside," said Mom. "You need to do all those things to get balance in your life."

"Hmmm," said Sophie. "Let me think about it."

The next day, Sophie decided to call Lily. "Do you still want to color?" she asked.

"Sure," said Lily. "Come to my house, and we can have milk and cookies in my backyard too."

Sophie spent all morning at Lily's. When it was time to leave, she said, "It was really fun being with you, Lily. You're a good friend, and you made my heart feel good too."

Later that day, Sophie went to Jumper's house. "My body needs exercise," she said. "Do you want to ride bikes now?"

"Oh, yeah! Oh, yeah!" said Jumper. "Let's ride!"

After Sophie and Jumper biked around 7 Oaks, Sophie said, "Thanks, Jumper, I really enjoyed the workout. My body feels better, and I feel balance coming into my life. Let's do this again sometime."

"Awesome!" said Jumper.

Now I have to think of something good for my soul,
thought Sophie. *I want to listen to music and watch the*
clouds. Where's Pokey?

Sophie found Pokey lying in his hammock.

"I'm ready to go to the lake and hear your new tune
now," Sophie said.

When they got to Fish-Eye Lake, Pokey played his
harmonica. Sophie lay in the grass and looked at the clouds.
She let her mind drift. She thought about butterflies. She
thought about flowers. She thought about going home.

"Thanks, Pokey," she said. "Your music was good for my soul. But now I have to go."

After Sophie got home, her mother asked, "How was your day?"

"Balanced!" said Sophie. "I used my heart when I colored with Lily, I used my body when I biked with Jumper, and I listened to Pokey's music with my soul. I'm feeling much better. But now I need to relax."

"Relax how?" asked Mom.

"It's time to use my mind again," said Sophie. "I think I'll go read a book!"

PARENTS' CORNER
Habit 7—Sharpen the Saw • *Balance Feels Best*

At times, my kids become grouchy or hyperactive, or literally start falling apart. I often overreact to their behavior by telling them to "stop acting like little kids," forgetting that they are just that. But my wife knows better. She realizes that it's usually a case of the kids being out of balance. They're tired, hungry, or overstimulated. So she'll feed them an apple, give them a bath, or read them a book until they turn "normal" again. The same principle applies to us adults, don't you think? We all feel better when we're balanced, when we take time to renew the four parts of who we are: body, heart, mind, and soul.

In this story, be sure to point out to the kids that just as a car has four tires, we, as people, also have four parts. And to be healthy and happy, all four parts need time and attention. Sophie got so focused on only one part, exercising her mind through books, that she neglected the other parts—her body, heart, and soul. That's why she felt so lethargic. Habit 7—Sharpen the Saw is all about finding that balance. Let us never be too busy sawing to take time to sharpen the saw.

Up for Discussion

1. Why did Sophie fall asleep during class? What did Sammy think the problem was?
2. When Sophie got home from school, what did she do? Who came over to play with her? Why didn't she want to play?
3. What did Sophie's mom tell Sophie she needed to do to feel better?
4. What did Sophie do that made her feel better?
5. Why is balance important?

Baby Steps

1. For two nights in a row, go to bed early and see how great you feel when you wake up!
2. For one whole week, read for twenty minutes every day.
3. Today go play with someone who you haven't played with for a long time.
4. Go to one of your favorite spots in nature, like a mountain, a park, or a stream. When you get there, think about all the things in your life that make you happy, like your grandma, your dog, a fun toy, or playing with your friends.

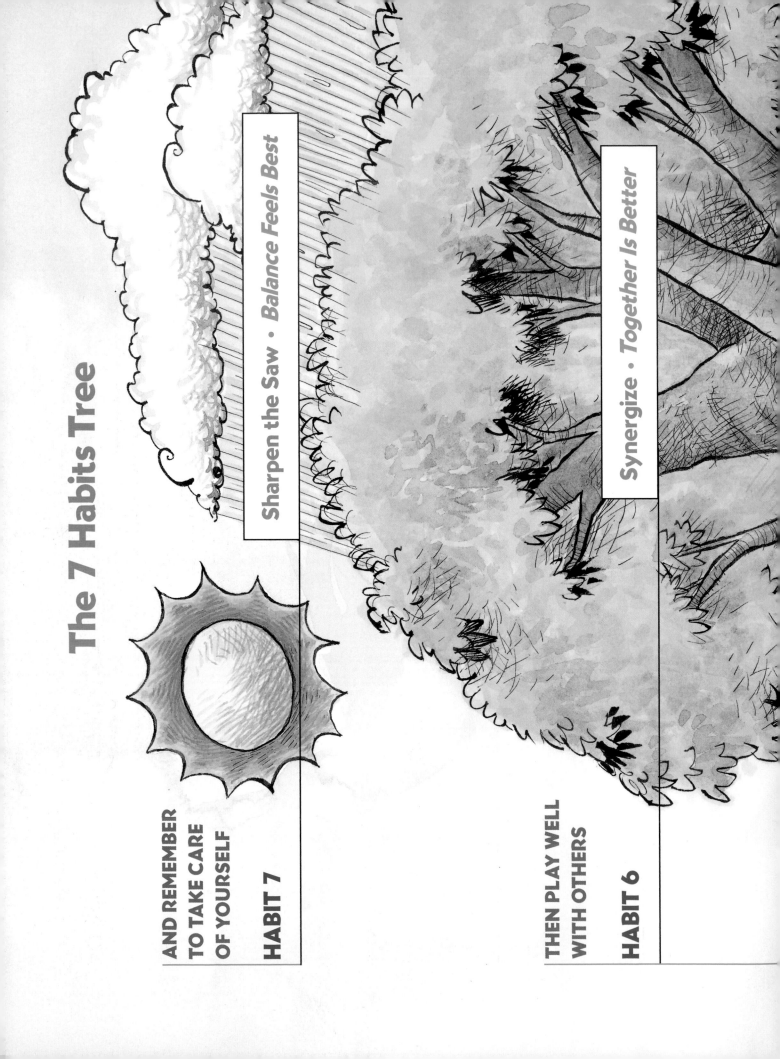

The 7 Habits Tree

Sharpen the Saw · *Balance Feels Best*

Synergize · *Together Is Better*

AND REMEMBER
TO TAKE CARE
OF YOURSELF

HABIT 7

THEN PLAY WELL
WITH OTHERS

HABIT 6

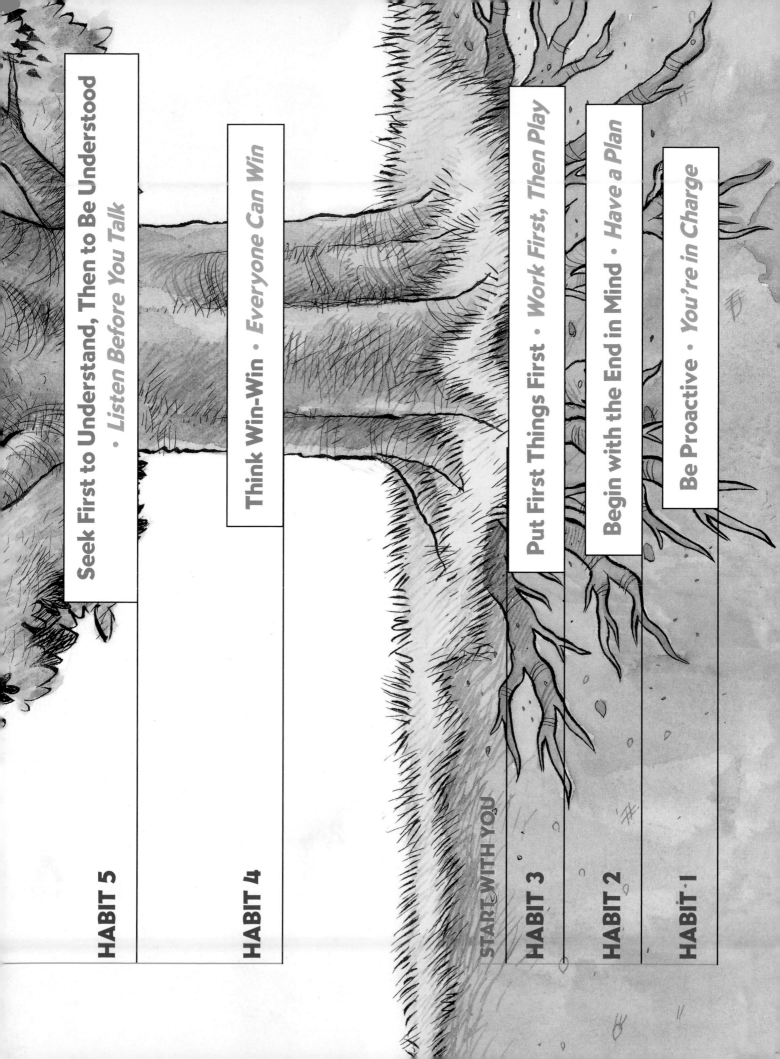

HABIT 5

Seek First to Understand, Then to Be Understood

· *Listen Before You Talk*

HABIT 4

Think Win-Win · *Everyone Can Win*

START WITH YOU

HABIT 3

Put First Things First · *Work First, Then Play*

HABIT 2

Begin with the End in Mind · *Have a Plan*

HABIT 1

Be Proactive · *You're in Charge*

A Note from Stephen R. Covey

Our son Sean, the author of this book for kids, was such a delightful child that when he went off to his first day of kindergarten in Hawaii (I was on sabbatical at the time), my wife cried: "I don't want him to go. He's such good company!" Sean wasn't too happy about going to Laie Elementary either. We struggled to even get him in the car. He was totally addicted to the nearby Hawaiian beaches and his barefooted lifestyle, and school was the furthest thing from his mind.

He has come a long way since then.

As a father, grandfather, and now great-grandfather, I have seen the profound influence that teaching timeless principles can have on people, particularly young children. That is why I commend to you this book, *The 7 Habits of Happy Kids*. It teaches the principles or natural laws embodied in the 7 Habits in an entertaining way that speaks directly to kids.

In today's world, we hear a lot about identity theft, where a thief gains access to your financial accounts and the like. What a misfortune. But there is a more serious type of identity theft going on and we're largely unaware of it. It happens when children forget who they really are and are stripped of their intrinsic worth and potential. This is the worst kind of identity theft.

When children are immersed in timeless, universal principles—such as responsibility, service, and honesty—both at home and at school, their tremendous worth and potential is affirmed and reinforced. They develop confidence, integrity, and the courage to do the right thing. They build character. And they get in touch with their real DNA.

On the other hand, if children are not taught true principles and don't see them modeled, they will grow up with comparison-based identities. In other words, they get their sense of self-worth, or lack thereof, from how well they stack up compared to others. As a result, peer pressure becomes their DNA (a cultural-versus-real DNA, if you will) and they lose self-confidence, integrity, and courage. They become more concerned with their image than with themselves and are thus robbed of their real identity.

Hence, the importance of constantly teaching and modeling correct principles!

I am thrilled that the adventures of Goob, Lily, Jumper, and the rest of the gang in 7 Oaks will reach our little ones. And I am stunned at how easy it is to learn the principles of the 7 Habits in the first eight years of life, rather than later, when kids develop comparison-based identities that are based on peers rather than principles.

Let us never forget that primary greatness is character; secondary greatness is popularity, prestige, and "success." Relatively few people have both. I know you want the children you are raising or teaching to have both, but of course, primary greatness is and should be first and foremost. After all, character is destiny. In the words of Daniel Webster:

"If we work upon marble, it will perish. If we work upon brass, time will efface it. If we rear temples, they will crumble to dust. But if we work upon immortal minds, and instill into them just principles, we are then engraving upon that tablet that which no time will efface, but will brighten and brighten to all eternity."

—Stephen R. Covey